T0199175

God's Colorful Palette

THE ARTFUL HUES OF ANIMALS, NATURE AND HUMANKIND

RITA CECILIA HUIE

WestBow Press books may be ordered through booksellers or by contacting:

WestBow Press
A Division of Thomas Nelson & Zondervan
1663 Liberty Drive
Bloomington, IN 47403
www.westbowpress.com
844-714-3454

Scripture quotations taken from The Holy Bible, New International Version® NIV® Copyright © 1973 1978 1984 2011 by Biblica, Inc. TM. Used by permission. All rights reserved worldwide.

ISBN: 978-1-6642-2567-1 (sc)
ISBN: 978-1-6642-2568-8 (e)

Library of Congress Control Number: 2021904467

Print information available on the last page.

WestBow Press rev. date: 03/31/2021

WESTBOW
PRESS®
A DIVISION OF THOMAS NELSON
& ZONDERVAN

Dedication

For Kaylee, Arya, Collin & Leah

The Hands of God and Adam by Michelangelo. He was one of the greatest sculptors in the world.

When God created Adam He designed him to look like Him. "So God created mankind in his own image..." (from Genesis 1:27 NIV). But nobody knows what Adam really looked like because there were no photographs. It didn't matter anyway, because that was a very, very long time ago.

When God said, "Let there be light," there was light. (from Genesis 1:3), He noticed something spectacular. The sun caused reflections of many beautiful colors and of each color there were shades of colors called hues, just like the paint strips in a paint store.

God decided to color and design all of the fish in the oceans and the lakes using many different colorful hues. "So God created the great creatures of the sea…"(Genesis 1:21). There were little gold fish and long shiny fish and huge dolphins and whales.

He then created and decorated multiple breeds of birds with feathers and different types of beaks to eat different things. "... and let birds fly above the earth across the vault of the sky" (Genesis 1:20). He made tiny hummingbirds with brilliant colors and long skinny beaks to drink out of flowers, and giant golden eagles with huge wingspans to fly above the mountains. He made sea birds and sparrows and doves and song birds.

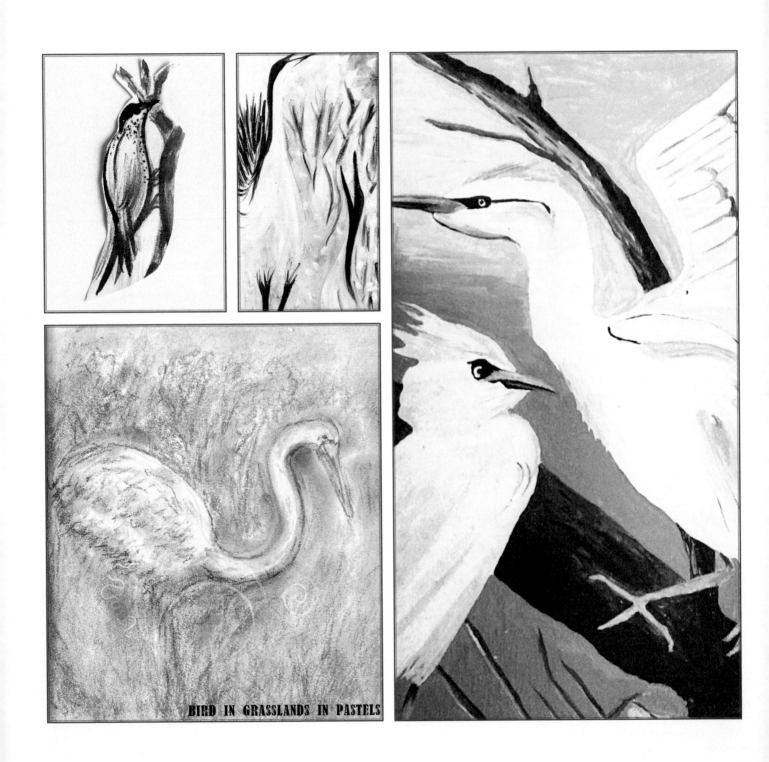

BIRD IN GRASSLANDS IN PASTELS

He designed so many animals and plants and trees and grasses I wonder if He lost count! He made bushes with small leaves and trees with big leaves in the jungle for shady umbrellas. He shaped dark green Christmas pine trees so we could decorate them.

MANY SHADES OF GREEN

CHRISTMAS PINES TO DECORATE

10

He gave cougars and leopards and some horses and cows dots, spots, blobs and ink blots. He gave sheep and other furry animals wool coats of many colors. "God made the wild animals according to their kinds, the livestock according to their kinds..." (Genesis 1:24).

ANIMAL PATTERNS

Flowers were made of every color, shape, size and texture. Even the clouds were shaded with pastels as they changed according to the weather. Every species was designed to adapt to the environment where He placed them. He had trouble staying with just one type of color for all of the living things because He loved all of the colors. He was so creative that some animals could change colors just as some trees would change colors according to the seasons.

STILL LIFE PHOTO
COLOR THE FLOWER USING A LIGHT PASTEL

MAGNOLIA IN OIL
PAINTS

USE MAGAZINE CUTOUTS + DRAWINGS FOR A NATURE COLLAGE

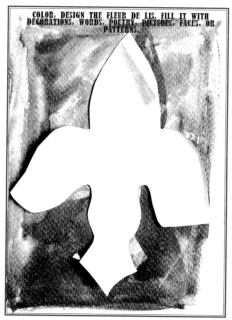

COLOR, DESIGN THE FLEUR DE LIS, FILL IT WITH
DECORATIONS, WORDS, POETRY, PICTURES, FACES, OR
PATTERNS.

Then God decided to color the people using many hues of colors on his palette. He mixed and blended and started to paint portraits of all the people. Because it would be too boring to have all living things the same color, He made one human form of people, but with many colorful hues. Since variety is the essence of creativity, God was having a lot of fun with designs and decoration.

Draw, design and color faces.

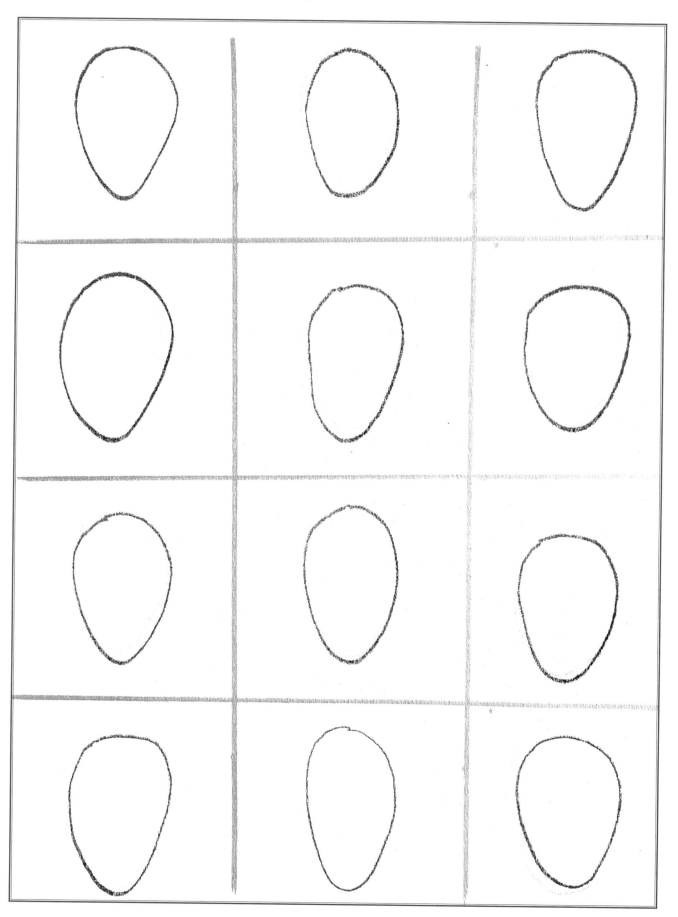

Then God realized the weather was different in all parts of the world so He designed the people to match the environments. In very hot places, skin types were tough and strong and able to stand the hot sun. In very cool places, skin types were adaptable to very cold weather. This is how it was with animals and plants too. Some flowers do not grow well in extreme heat or in extreme cold, and some birds thrive in the jungle while others walk along the beach or in the snow. He decided it should be the same for the many skin types of the peoples.

And so all of the people in the world had various skin tones according to God's great palette. He felt joy painting portraits of all of His different people. And the people had children and their children had children, and so on and on, so that the colors mixed and blended automatically by this thing called genetics. Eye color and hair colors, size, shape and height are all from genetics. You can find genetics in your family tree! God became tired, so He allowed genetics to take over the process. Then God could take a rest from all of this art work while other artists began to paint portraits and create sculptures.

Van Gogh was a Dutch Impressionist artist who painted many colors of stripes on each of his Portraits. *Self Portrait*, 1887. Color the stripes differently.

Queen Nefertiti was an Egyptian bust made out of clay around 1370. Color and decorate.

The Thinker, Le Penseur, is a sculpture made of bronze made by French Sculptor Auguste Rodin around 1902. Color him any color. What is he thinking about?

Ancient Africans made masks out of wood. Draw, color and
design and decorate the mask.

Pablo Picasso, famous Spanish artist developed Cubism. *Self Portrait*, 1907. Color each shape using several hues.

Your shade of skin tone comes from a long, interesting history of people from places all over the world. Where did your families come from? Some people came from South America, Cuba or Mexico. Others came from England, France, Spain or Italy. Some people came from China, Japan, the Philippines, or Vietnam. Some people became cowboys in the old west. Many Native Americans were already settled in different parts of the Americas. There were African tribes, Japanese Samurai, and Islanders who wore elaborate costumes. There were strong builders who built the pyramids of Egypt. There were warriors and Vikings and Soldiers and Kings and Queens. There were so many different cultures!

Viking, African Mask, Mexican Warrior, Samurai

Cowboy, Spanish Queen, Native Headdress

Label the Pears for Your Family Tree

Your Family Tree of Life

Everyone has a different family tree and everyone of every color and every language and every nationality is the same in God's eyes just like the animals, birds, fish, flowers and trees are all equal in importance and beauty. This is true because it was His design. The world is very big and there are lots of colors everywhere. But one thing is for sure, we are all one people although we all look different. All of the colors of the world and the many hues and tones of skin are beautiful because God was the finest artist and the most creative artist of all.

Yet you, Lord, are our Father. We are the clay, you are the potter; we are all the work of your hand. Isaiah 64:8

Add family faces to this tree

Family Tree

Add family faces to this tree

Family Tree

I can paint myself in any color. Self Portrait by the author/artist.

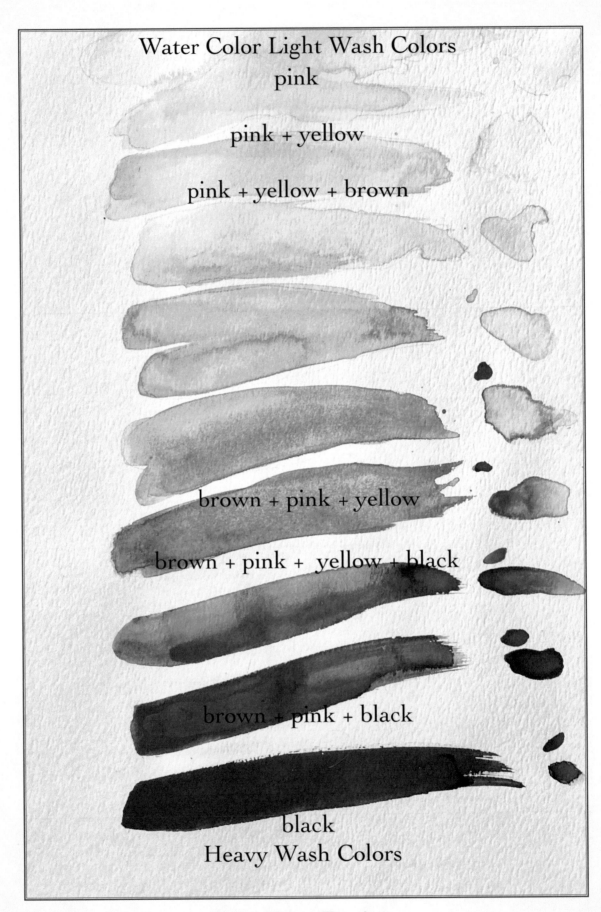

Water Color Light Wash Colors
pink

pink + yellow

pink + yellow + brown

brown + pink + yellow

brown + pink + yellow + black

brown + pink + black

black
Heavy Wash Colors

Skin Tone Recipes

HUES FOR OIL PORTRAITS

RAW UMBER
CRIMSON
BURNT SIENNA
VIOLET
BRIGHT RED
BRILLIANT RED
ORANGE
PEACH
YELLOW OCHRE
LEMON YELLOW
ZINC WHITE
TITANIUM WHITE
MIXING WHITE
UNBLEACHED WHITE
PAYNE'S GRAY

Printed in the United States
by Baker & Taylor Publisher Services